MW00760168

PRAISE FOR THE POEMS

J.R. Solonche can pack so much humor and linguistic playfulness into such tight bundles, it feels like 1,000 clowns issuing from a VW Bug. He can also fit a lot of darkness and mortality into them, which feels more like 1,000 clowns dressed like Marilyn Mason issuing from a VW Bug. Solonche can be crass the way only the truthful can be, mischievous as a child with his hands in the honey jar, or even aphoristic and proverbial like a modern day Martial. Though you never know which Solonche you're going to encounter on the next page, he's a great bunch of guys to get to know.

— Stephen Cramer is the winner of the Louise Bogan Award and the National Poetry Series

The history of book blurbs is littered with high falutin' praise, whacky and wild metaphors, written to impress not to inform. All I need to say about J.R. Solonche's poems is that they are good, really, really good. So much so that they have a high "I-wish-I'd-written-that" factor. That's a compliment I hand out to very few poets writing today. You want wit? You want humor? You want erudition? You want them all mixed into poems? Try Solonche. You won't be disappointed. Envious perhaps, but not disappointed.

— John Murphy is editor of *The Lake Contemporary Poetry Webzine*

In a style that favors brevity and pith, J.R. Solonche brings a richness of experience, observation, and wit into his poems. Here is the world! they exclaim. And here and here and here! Watched over by ancient lyric gods – Time, Death, and Desire— we find the quotidian here transformed.

— Christopher Nelson is editor of Green Linden Press

Sample one by one these epigrammatic, epiphenomenal, Epicurean episodes as if they were puffs from a tower of pastry. Savor the zest of lemon, the pinch of sea salt, the dollop of crème fraiche, and the absence of any more sugar than necessary to ease the ingestion of truth. A feast for fanatics of language and lovers of pith. I'm not sure what pith is, but I know it when I see it.

— Sarah White is author most recently of I*ridescent Guest*

The best feature of Solonche's poetry is its diversity. Everyone who encounters this volume (including the postman who delivers it to you) will find something in it to understand and remember—and a great deal to enjoy.

— Tony Beyer is author of *Anchor Stone*, finalist for the New Zealand Book Award.

A Guide of the Perplexed

Poems

J.R. Solonche

SERVING
HOUSE
BOOKS

BOOKS BY J.R. SOLONCHE

CONTENTS

THE GUIDE FOR THE PERPLEXED

When I was nineteen or twenty,
I started to read
The Guide for the Perplexed
by Moses Maimonides.
I was nineteen or twenty.
I was perplexed.
I needed a guide.
I read a few pages
by the great Jewish sage.
Perhaps I read a chapter.
I don't remember.
But I soon realized I needed
a guide to the guide.
I have never gone back to read
what was next
in *The Guide for the Perplexed*
by Moses Maimonides.
It's not my fault.
He should have illustrated the text
with pictures of flowers.
Roses and tulips and daisies.
Or just a little sex.

IT WAS QUIET

It was quiet.
The only voice was the crow's.
It was in the top of the tree behind me.
It was speaking from the heart.
"Listen, I am speaking from the heart," it said.
"But don't you always speak from the heart?" I said.
"Yes, I do," it said.
"But you do not always listen from the heart."
It flew off.
It was quiet again.

THE SNOW MELTS

The snow melts.
It drips from the eaves.
From the branches of the trees.
A dog barks.
Soon the sun will be gone.
Soon it will be forgotten.
Soon the sun will be gone.
A dog barks.
From the branches of the trees.
It drips from the eaves.
The snow melts.

DECEMBER

The wet, weighty snow
has overweighed
the rhododendron and broken
off its biggest branch,
which lies on the ground,
happy somehow with
nothing more to do.

AMERICA

The notebook I am writing in was made in China
The pen I am writing with was made in China.
The chair I am sitting on was made in China.
The desk I am sitting at was made in China.
The frames of the glasses I am seeing with were made in China.
The glass I am drinking from was made in China.
But the bourbon I am drinking was made in America.
And the poem I am writing was made in America.
And that's enough America for me.

IT ALL DEPENDS ON DEPENDENCY

It all depends on who remembers the name.
It all depends on who is around to see.
It all depends on the last move of the game.
It all depends on the oral history of history.

It all depends on the differences of the same.
It all depends on the courage of anonymity.
It all depends on whose freedom is to blame.
It all depends on the difference of degree.

It all depends on the better part of shame.
It all depends on the mood of memory.
It all depends on the fickleness of fame.
It all depends on the wild cherry tree.

It all depends on who forgets the name.
It all depends on A B C.
It all depends on the flicker of a flame.
It all depends on possible probability.

It all depends on who never came.
It all depends on X Y Z.
It all depends on the flicker of a frame.
It all depends on probable possibility.

SONG

The woodpecker
in the tree behind
me is not singing
the woodpecker's
song. He is singing
the song of the tree.

THE POWER

If you had the power,
would you change the world,
or would you grow a single silver flower?

If you had the power,
would you change the world,
or would you add a single silver hour?

If you had the power,
would you change the world,
or would you build a single silver tower?

If you had the power,
would you change the world,
or would you bring a single silver shower?

THERE IS JUST ENOUGH SUN

There is just enough sun
angling late in to show
the wild cherry's shadow
on the house's side like
a black and white movie
shown in slow motion
slowed to the slowest
motion that can be
possibly shown.

WHEN THE WIND STOPS

When the wind stops,
the leaves stop falling
while those already
fallen stop skittering
along the ground and
pause before the cul-de-
sacs of wall and fence
or fence and shed or shed
and steps or steps and wall.

A HAWK

A hawk has not been
moving at the top of
the tall dead tree across
the road for a long time.
It looks like what I would
like to look like when
I am daydreaming on top
of my favorite bench
in the park.

GRAY

It is all overcast.
The clouds, all of them,
are cast over
the sun so there are no shadows
anywhere, yet everywhere is shadow.
Let the sun shine or let it rain, I say.
The middle ground is no firm ground.
Give me one end or the other.
Gray is gray is gray is gray.

THE DOGS

The dogs are barking.
All the dogs within a mile
it seems are barking. Ah,
I know why. It's a quarter
after three. All the kids
are getting home from school.

WHEN I ASKED

When I asked,
he didn't know
the first thing
about it. This
is very bad, for
one thing is all
there ever is to
know about it.

THE SUN

The sun is slow.
It takes its sweet time.

Why shouldn't it?
It has nowhere to go.

It is slow.
It makes the night wait.

It makes the dark curse behind its back.
It makes the stars grit their teeth.

UNTIL SPRING IS TRUE

The ice thaws.
The snow melts.

Their waters mingle and run as one.
The birds sing, "Let us be false to one another."

The turtles that slumber in the mud meanwhile
at the swamp's bottom will not awaken.

They dream on.
The sun may be cruel, but it is not that cruel.

THE DELIVERY

The UPS driver delivered
a boxful of my new book.
I gave him one. "You're
a writer?" he said. "No,"
I said. "I'm a poet." "Oh,
is there a difference?" he
said. "Yes, writers write to
be understood. Poets write
to be remembered," I said.
"Well, I'll remember you,"
he said. "Good," I said.
"Also it couldn't hurt
to understand what you
remember." "Got it," he said.

UNSEASONABLE

It is so warm, a spider
has awakened. It will not
get far before the cold comes
back, but bless its heart, that
spider will get far enough
to get to its very own Florida
in the grass, which is a lot
farther than I will ever get.

SWAN

Before I caught sight
of the white folded back
wing and the white neck,
flash of white light and
flash of white light
through the trees by
the shallow end of the lake,
I had anything but
swans on my mind,
but all day I have been
thinking about that swan,
wondering if I were to
be one which kind
of swan I would choose
to be always, since I,
by choice or not,
myself have known,
depending on my season,
what it means to be
both whistling and mute.

NOW THAT IT'S THREE O'CLOCK

Now that it's three o'clock,
I wish this were a civilized country.

Now that it's three o'clock,
I wish this were Moorish Spain,

where the Christians, Muslims and Jews
lived together in peace and harmony.

Now that it's three o'clock,
I wish this were a civilized country

where the Christians, the Muslims and the Jews drank wine,
wrote poems and talked philosophy far into the night.

Now that it's three o'clock,
I wish this were a civilized country.

THE WINDOW SHADE: A PROSE POEM WITH TWO ENDINGS

I had a neighbor once who was a psychologist. His office was in his house. It was easy to see through the window. Whenever he had a new patient, the very first thing he did was ask if the patient wanted the shade up or down. He said this immediately gave him the first glimpse into the patient's psyche. If the patient wanted the shade up, he was probably dealing with an exhibitionist. If the patient wanted the shade down, he knew he had an introvert, or worse, on his hands. In any case, a patient with something to hide. "Did you ever have a patient who wanted the shade halfway?" I asked. "Actually, yes, there was one. She turned out to be schizoid," he said. "Did she get better?" I asked. "Yes, but it took a couple of years," he said. I started to tell him something. That when I walk on the road at night, all the shades are up. Except the office shade, which is down. I changed my mind and didn't mention it. I don't know why. That's not true. I do know why. But I won't say. *That when I walk on the road at night, all the shades are down. Except the office shade, which is up. I changed my mind and didn't mention it. I don't know why. That's not true. I do know why, but I won't say.*

CHRISTMAS

One of my neighbors is playing
Christmas music. It is very loud.
I hear Bing Crosby. I hear Dinah
Shore. I hear Johnny Mathis.
I hear Brenda Lee. I hear *Feliz
Navidad.* I want to tell him to
turn down the volume. I want
to tell him the whole neighborhood
can hear it. But I'm not going to
tell him to turn the volume down.
This is the only time he plays
music this loud. He doesn't do it
on July Fourth. He doesn't even do
it on New Year's Eve. At least it's
not the Mormon Tabernacle Choir.

ANTHROPO IS THE ONLY MORPHISM WE KNOW

Do you understand the difference between
the moon and the meaning of the moon?

Do you understand the difference between
the crow and the meaning of the crow?

Do you understand the difference between
the ash tree and the meaning of the ash tree?

Do you understand the difference between
the fox and the meaning of the fox?

Do you understand the difference between
the lake and the meaning of the lake?

Do you understand the difference between
the snake and the meaning of the snake?

Do you understand the difference between
the mountain and the meaning of the mountain?

Do you understand the difference between
the wind and the meaning of the wind?

Do you understand the difference between
the woman and the meaning of the woman?

GARDENS

The plaque reads, *Planted to Honor*
Professor John De Nicolo, Given by
His Colleagues and Friends, but it is
so overgrown, the plants so entangled
one with the other, one cannot tell
just what was planted here to honor
Professor John De Nicolo. Some
would say it doesn't really matter.
I think I'm one of those. So plant one
for me, dear colleagues and friends,
when the time comes, and let it grow
to overgrown, and let the flowers
and the weeds become so entangled
one with the other, one cannot tell
just what you planted here to honor me.
It will be a garden. For what's-his-name.

LAST NIGHT I HAD A DREAM

Last night I had a dream that I was drafted. I was in the army. I wasn't nineteen in my dream. I was what I am now. I was seventy-three. I had a wife, I had a daughter. I was on a bus with the other draftees, all seventy-year-old men with wives and daughters, and all whose names began with *S*. The bus was full. It was a bus only for us seventy-year-old men with wives and daughters and names that began with *S*. We were talking about where we were going. *To Iraq,* said one draftee of seventy with wife and daughter whose name began with *S*. *To Afghanistan,* said another draftee of seventy with wife and daughter whose name began with *S*. *No, to South America, I heard,* said another draftee of seventy with wife and daughter whose name began with *S*. *He's right. We're going to invade Venezuela,* said another draftee of seventy with wife and daughter whose name began with *S*. *Yeah, that's what I heard too, to topple Chavez and get the oil before he gives it all away to the poor countries,* said another draftee of seventy with wife and daughter whose name began with *S*. When I woke up I didn't care who was right. It didn't mean anything. It didn't bother me. Why should it? It was a dream. Unless that wasn't me I was dreaming about. Unless that was my daughter I was dreaming about. Unless those were our daughters we were dreaming about.

TO A WOODCHUCK

Somebody got you.
It was inevitable.

Such a busy road.
So much traffic.

How fast they whiz by.
Faster than the sign says they should.

And not everyone can be as alert as I was.
As quick to react when I nearly got you coming the other way.

You should have learned your lesson.
But you didn't.

Maybe you should have gotten your nose bloodied.
That's how I learned.

That's how I learned about whom to cross,
and about whom not to cross when I was growing up.

But you didn't.
And now look at you.

Your nose is bleeding.
And you're dead.

POLAR BEARS

Dying off. That's what's happening.
They're dying off. How can this be happening?
Their kingdom of ice, their white continent,
their fortress, their palace, their world,
it is melting, it is dissolving around them,
it is disappearing out from under them,
and they are drowning in it, the solitary males
and the females with their cubs, they are all
drowning in it, this desert of water whose
distances now are too far for them to swim
so they tire and drown in it, this iceless sea
with no solidity that we have made of their
kingdom of ice, not thick enough, not deep
enough, not strong enough to save them
from us. I cannot believe it, I cannot
believe what we are doing to them, what
we will have done to them when it is done,
to the polar bears, to the animals I could
not get enough of, in the Bronx Zoological
Garden, when my mother took me there
to see them, as I stood, with my hands
on the iron railing and cried out, "Look
at the white bears! They look like snow!",
and stood, awestruck, with my hands stuck
to the iron railing, just stood there and looked
at them, at the white bears, at the bears
that looked like snow, and looked at them
and looked at them and looked and looked.

AN EMPTY WASPS' NEST

An empty wasps' nest
hangs from a branch.

It laughs at the wind
as the wind passes

through it, and they both
laugh at me as I pass.

MY JAPANESE DEATH POEM

When I die, bury me
with an acorn
in my mouth.
Then at least one
of us might become
the mighty oak tree
that both our mothers
wanted done.

I WALK THE RAILROAD TRACKS

I walk the railroad tracks
with you as my mind's companion,

Galway Kinnell, your fellow Euclidean.
The tracks are straight here.

They point straight to where they vanish through the trees.
You were eighty-seven. I am seventy-three.

The prostate is enlarged, the arthritis worsening.
I'm on the way, all right.

Now, for the first time in my life, I see it, Galway.
I see the point in vanishing completely out of sight.

HYDRANGEA

It is the middle of January,
and the hydrangea, long dead,
is still standing tall. What will it
take to knock it off its feet?
Does it want to be around to greet
the new hydrangea come spring?
Yes, that's exactly what I think.

WHEN THE BREEZE BLOWS

When the breeze blows,
the trees speak up. They gossip.
They're abuzz with news.
"Long time, no hear," says the oak.
"What's up with you?" says the pine.
"See this crow? I hope it croaks.
Otherwise, I'm fine."

RED

We were in the bar. College basketball was on the big TV. Alabama versus Kentucky. "Kentucky will win," said Jim. "How do you know?" I said. "Alabama's wearing red." "And that's why Kentucky will win?" "Yep, that's why. Alabama's red uniforms will make Kentucky see red. It'll pump up their testosterone," Jim said. "It's the psychology of color." "Interesting. I guess that explains why St. Valentine's Day's color is always red." "Yes," he said. "It's always red lingerie. Red roses. Also why a Ferrari is sexiest in red." "So why didn't you marry a redhead?" I said. "I almost did," Jim said. "You never told me that. What happened?" I said. "She wasn't natural. She dyed her hair red. She had black roots," Jim said. "That's tough," I said. "Gee." "Yeah," Jim said. "Hey, look," I said. "Alabama won. Sorry."

WASHING MACHINE

Someone put a Samsung
washing machine out
to be picked up. I guess
it doesn't work, but it looks
new. It gleams in the sun.
Its white gleams whiter
than a sugar cube in the sun.
Its white gleams whiter
than an iceberg in the sun.
Its white gleams whiter
than a clean sheet in the sun.
"Come here," it sings to me.
"Come and open my crystal
door, my magical door,"
it sings to me. "Come here
and I will absolve you of
your sins," it sings to me.
"I will wash you through
and through, whiter than white,
cleaner than clean," it sings.
And I believe it. I really do.

AFTER THE DOWNPOUR

After the downpour,
the sun pours down
unabated all day,
playing the geese
on the lake with
its silver line and
its golden hook.

BEHIND

What now is
just right behind
will almost always
eventually be
just left behind.

A STORY

Once upon a time, there was a story.
It had a normal and uneventful childhood.
When it reached adulthood, it left home.
It went out into the world in search of someone to tell it.
It searched and searched.
It grew old searching without finding anyone to tell it.
Approaching the end, it returned to its birthplace where it died and was eaten by crows.
The crows flew off in all four directions of the world, telling its story in four different ways.

SO I SHALL SHAVE

So I shall need a shave.
So I shall wet my face at the sink.
So I shall lather my face with soap.
So I shall take up the disposable razor.
So I shall scrape the razor down and across and over my face.
So the sharp blade of the razor shall remove the hair from my face.
So I shall rinse my face with clean water.
So I shall rinse out the sink.
So the hairs of my face shall go down the drain.
So I shall feel my smooth face with my fingers.
So I shall go out to face the world with my face.
So I shall not feel ashamed of my face.
So I shall not be the subject of pity from my neighbors.
So I shall not be the subject of suspicion from the police officers.
So I shall not have to answer the question, "Growing a beard?"
So I shall not have to suffer the frowns of the attractive women in town.
Oh, yes, I shall shave.

BREAKFAST

I eat oatmeal for breakfast.
Sometimes I eat oat bran.
Just for the sake of a little variety.
Unlike Kinnell, I do not invite John Keats to eat breakfast with me.
Did John Keats even eat breakfast?
He was tubercular.
So he didn't eat much at all.
His favorite food was roast beef sandwiches.
Walter Scott said that cold roast beef was the ideal breakfast dish.
Keats probably knew that.
So, no, I would not think Keats ate oatmeal.
It doesn't matter.
I've always preferred Coleridge over Keats, anyway.
And Blake over both.
I drink coffee standing at the kitchen window.
I once wondered why oatmeal is one word while oat bran is two words.
I researched it, but couldn't find out.
I look at the birds eat breakfast at the feeders.
I do not invite John Keats.
I eat breakfast alone.
The way breakfast should be eaten.
The way Blake ate breakfast while watching the angels through his window.

THE MOST BEAUTIFUL POEM IN THE ENGLISH LANGUAGE

According to William R. Espy, the ten most beautiful words in the English language are *gonorrhea, gossamer, lullaby, meandering, mellifluous, murmuring, onomatopoeia, Shenandoah, summer afternoon,* and *wisteria. (The Book of Lists)*

On a summer afternoon,
meandering along the Shenandoah,
smelling the wisteria,
murmuring a mellifluous onomatopoeia
lullaby to a beautiful lady in gossamer,
I contracted gonorrhea.

HARRIER

As the harrier, harried,
hurries in surprise
in the channel of
shed and house,
a wind-fluster strips
its tail stripes
across the grass
to accost an oak.

LEAVES, TEXTURE , A PHOTOGRAPH BY GEORGE SAINES

What is this black
and white fall
other than a fall
for the blind,
a Braille fall?
Winter of fall,
this Autumn,
so colorless, so
formal in black tie.
The oak leaves,
bleached to the bone,
piled against a fence
whiter than the whitest
white picket fence
of a newlywed's dreams,
and the oak tree
from which they fell,
burned black in
the furnace of color,
is the shadow of fall.

ANOTHER BIG CHANGE

Joy, who is 22 and finally their sister.
They are getting used to it.
Even when the lesson changes.

At night when the sky is black.
From living in the city where they
had friends across the street.

From lions to peacock to camels, they said.
Bright sun. Fresh air. Lots of play.
For the simple reason that they couldn't afford it.

Joy, who is 22 and finally their sister.
The whole idea.
The neighbor who lived next door.

They hated each other.
Joy, who is 22 and finally their sister.
Not another big change.

CIGARS

My father smoked White Owls.
They had little red paper rings around them.
The rings had the picture of a white owl.

I never asked my father what cigars had to do with owls.
I think I already knew that owls didn't smoke cigars.
But I grew up thinking that all owls in the world were white.

They were cheap.
They stank.
My mother told him to smoke them in the street.

Then he smoked Dutch Masters.
They had little gold paper rings around them.
The rings had the picture of a Dutch master.

I didn't know what a Dutch master was.
He had a neatly groomed beard and a big black hat.
He also had a weird collar around his neck.

He looked like a flower.
I thought he was a fag.
They were cheap, too.

They stank.
My mother told him to smoke them in the street.
Finally he smoked Garcia y Vega.

They had little silver rings around them.
The rings had the picture of a Spanish lady.
I didn't know if she was a senora or a senorita.

I never asked my father about this.
I also never asked if her name was Garcia or if it was Vega.
Or why the cigars had two names with only one lady on the rings.

Garcia y Vegas were my favorites.
I liked the box they came in.
The lid had the same picture only bigger.

I put stuff in the empty boxes he gave me.
They weren't so cheap.
They didn't stink as much.

But my mother told him to smoke them in the street.
One day my father died of a heart attack.
He was smoking in the street.

He was smoking one of those.
He was smoking a Garcia y Vega.
Oh, Garcia. Oh, Vega.

COMMONALITY

The blood of the horseshoe
crab is blue. This is because it
is copper not iron that carries
the oxygen in the bloodstream
of horseshoe crabs. This is the
sort of fact that only a biologist
or a poet could love.

THIS MUST BE IT

This must be it,
the only sonnet
he ever wrote, that
starts "nude bodies
are like peeled logs" and
ends with the couplet
"has no odor, odor of
a nude woman sometimes,
odor of a man," Williams,
William Carlos, who hated
the sonnet, who said it
was a crab you had to cut
the legs off to fit
in the box, or something such,
the one called *Sonnet
in Search of an Author.*

ODYSSEUS!

Odysseus!
You're our man.
Yours is the war we wanted to find our glory in.

Odysseus!
You're our man.
Yours is the sea we wanted to journey home on.

Odysseus!
You're our man.
Yours is the wife we wanted faithful to us.

Odysseus!
You're our man.
 Yours is the dog we wanted drowsy by our door.

Odysseus!
You're our man.
 Yours is the song we wanted to sing in our memories.

Odysseus!
You're our man.
Yours are the rope burns we wanted on our arms and wrists.

Odysseus!
You're our man.
Yours is the epic we wanted for our piece of the pie.

ON THE LOWER ROOF

On the lower roof,
a sharp-shinned hawk
could not ride out
last night's storm.
Wet to the bone,
weighed down
down to earth by wind
and rain, how much
less hawk dead he is
than when he lorded
over every roof around.
Pity, pity that I have seen
one such thing that life
should have no business
letting anyone see.

ON WHY THERE'S NO MONUMENT IN WASHINGTON D.C. TO JOHN ADAMS

Well, let's see. There's one
to Washington, slave owner,
ethnic cleanser, and the richest
citizen in the new free free-enterprise
America. There's one to Jefferson,
slave owner, ethnic cleanser, and
adulterer. There's one to Lincoln,
reluctant slave emancipator, ethnic
cleanser, and rail splitting fence-sitter.
So why is there none to Adams?
"Because," said my colleague in
the history department, "he was
a complete and utter asshole."

IN THE MIDDLE OF TIME

In the middle of time, when
you are not looking, but looking
at steel, grass, glass, iron, stone,
feather, wind, leaf, cloud, flesh,
blood, and it comes time to see
what you are made of, what will
you see you are made of? Steel?
Grass? Glass? Iron? Stone? Feather?
Wind? Leaf? Cloud? Flesh? Blood?

IN THE SUN

I asked the old fisherman
what he had caught, for
I saw that the rod he had stood
against the railing was curved
down, and the fishing line was taut.
"A turtle," he said. "A snapper."
"It isn't moving," I said. "No,"
he said. "He's in the grass.
I'll let him hang a while.
He's found a comfortable place
for himself. Just two old men
in the sun.""Three," I said,
shading my eyes with my hand.

ANGER

Merwin, at the reading you said
that anger ruins poems, that it is
next to impossible to write an
angry poem that's really any good,
and the only one you could think of
at the moment was number eleven
by Catullus, but I have to tell you,
I have written lots of angry poems
that are really good, and even one or
two very angry poems that are really
very good, but I can't send them to
you because they made me so angry
I tore them up and threw them away.

SOMEONE

Someone came up to me
after the reading. "Your
poems are very strange,"
she said. "Oh," I said.
"How so?" In the way
they sort of exist outside
of time," she said. "Why
is that strange? Aren't all
poems supposed to sort of
exist that way?" I said.
She had a beautiful smile.

THERE IS A BEAUTY AT THE BOTTOM OF THE BREATH

There is a beauty at the bottom of the breath
that sings the song of the one word richer than all the rest:
"Belong. Belong. Belong."

THERE IS A HOLE IN THE CLOUDS

There is a hole in the clouds that lets the sun
shine through at just the right angle
to look angelic.
I saw them just now, nodding in unison,
the two of them, lying to my face that way,
trying yet again
to get me to believe in their Hallmark heaven.
They never give up, those two, no matter what I say.

THERE IS A MOMENT THAT HAS NO USE FOR TIME

There is a moment that has no use for time.
There is a moment that neither looks behind nor ahead.
There is a moment that closes its eyes.
There is a moment that shuts its ears.
There is a moment that is one breath long.
There is a moment that has never heard of movement.
There is a moment that stands stock-still.
There is a moment that lives forever.
There is a moment that dies forever.
There is a moment whose name is *Eternity*.
There is a moment that does not answer to *Eternity*.
There is a moment that answers only to eternity.

THERE IS A BOOK THAT REFUSES TO BE WRITTEN

There is a book that refuses to be written.
There is a book with a spine made of steel.
There is a book whose pages are of silver.
There is a book that can be read only in moonlight.
There is a book that can be read only by near-sighted eyes.
There is a book that would rather die than be written.
There is a book too proud to be read.
There is a book that cannot keep a secret.
There is a book that wants to be a book that no one has read.
There is a book that wants its name on everyone's lips.
There is a book that wants to be sworn on.
There is a book that wants young ladies to swoon over.
There is a book that wants to be held in your hands.
There is a book that wants to be blank.
There is a book that says, "Keep your hands off me."
There is a book that wants to stare without blinking.
There is a book. There is a book. There is a book.

THERE IS A HOLE IN THE BLUE ABOVE ME

There is a hole in the blue above me.
A jet is jetting through it.
The jet is not making the hole.
The hole was there before the jet was there.
The hole was awaiting the arrival of the jet.
The hole was ready for the jet.
It was exactly the wingspan's width.
It was exactly the flight path's length.
How did the hole know this?
Ah, that is a mystery.
And who doesn't love a mystery?

THERE IS A POTHOLE IN THE ROAD

There is a pothole in the road.
The crew from the highway department is on the job.
They are filling the hole with hot asphalt.
There is fire.
There is smoke.
There is the smell of burning road.
There is the small taste of hell the road to which is paved with good intentions.

THERE IS A HOLE IN YOUR STORY

There is a hole in your story.
It is a peephole.
It is big enough for one eye only.
It is for a peep show for which one eye is sufficient.

THERE IS A HOLE IN THE OLD OAK TREE

There is a hole in the old oak tree.
Owls once nested in it.
That was years ago.
I heard the owlets inside.
One time the mother owl showed herself in the opening.
She fixed me with her eyes.
That was the one and only time.
For a week thereafter, I was fixed.
For a week thereafter, I was whole.

THERE IS A HOLE IN THE SOUL

There is a hole in the soul
into which I dare
not fall for fear
of meeting at the other side the anti-soul.

THE EYELIDS OF A WOMAN ARE THE MOST BEAUTIFUL PART OF THE WOMAN

The eyelids of a woman are the most beautiful part of the woman.
Every time I dream about kissing a woman,
I dream I am kissing the eyelids of the woman's closed eyes.
I do not know why.
Could it mean I am saying,
"Thank you, thank you, thank you for not seeing who I really am?"

THE MISTAKE THE MYSTICS MAKE

The mistake the mystics make is a small mistake.
It is this.
The mystics mistake the god for the goddess.
This is an understandable mistake.
It is a case of mistaken identity.
It doesn't take much to correct.
It takes only one dream to correct.
The same is true of reductionists.

PRINCETON

Princeton, where there are more churches than lecture halls.
Or do all the lecture halls look like churches?

What worshipful students at Princeton.
What a worshipful faculty at Princeton.

I watched a young mother with a baby in a stroller.
She was struggling to ascend the stairs of one of the churches.

This was a church, not a lecture hall.
Before I could offer my help, she was at the top.

She was beautiful.
She was beautifully dressed.

The stroller was beautifully appointed.
Her husband must be a doctor or a lawyer or a professor or an administrator.

I wanted to ask her, "Why are you going into this church?"
I wanted to ask her, "What do you want to pray for?"

I wanted to ask her, "Or do you just want to see the stained glass windows?"
It is true.

The stained glass windows are beautiful.
Even from the outside, the stained glass windows are beautiful at Princeton.

IF I COULD BRING MYSELF TO WORSHIP ANYTHING

If I could bring myself to worship anything,
it would be the sun, for it is the sun
that is the omnipotent one,
and omnipotence is all a god
needs to be one.
Omnipresence?
Omniscience?
Omnibenevolence?
They create nothing but confusion.
Especially the one that means, *All good*.

ONCE I WANTED A MIND

Once I wanted a mind
that could know
what the world was thinking.

Once I wanted eyes
that could see
right through to the very heart of things.

Once I wanted ears
that could hear
the secrets the stars whisper to one another.

Once I wanted feet
that could carry me
around the earth as swiftly as light.

Once I wanted a voice
that could sing
my song so loud the moon would hear.

Once I wanted a heart
so welcoming,
so giving, it would love all equally.

That was once.
Now my mind, my eyes, my ears, my feet,
my voice, my heart have better things to do.

WHEN THE SHADOWS ARE LONG

When the shadows are long,
my thoughts grow short. My
thoughts hurry back from
their excursions on the lake or
in the woods or on the hillsides.
They hurry back before the moon casts
its cold white darkness on the earth,
before the stars pluck out your eyes.

CLOTHES UNMAKE THE MAN

I am wearing jeans
and a tee shirt. What
kind of man do these
clothes make therefore?
A man who has no interest
in clothes? A man who has
no interest in what kind of
man he is? Shame on him.
Shame on him.

A CARDINAL

A cardinal has found
the rainwater in the birdbath.
How glad I am that I was
too lazy to carry it into
the shed as I had intended.

TREE STUMP

The big woodpecker
on the tree stump by
the road must have
thought I wanted
the tree stump too,
for he shouted out
warnings as I passed
and didn't believe me
when I assured him
I had no interest in
his kind of grub.

HAVE I BELITTLED THE SOUL FOR TOO LONG?

Have I belittled the soul for too long?
Yes, I have belittled the soul for too long.
Have I been unfair to the soul?
Yes, I have been unfair to the soul.
The soul is so little.
It's not fair.
The way I look down on it is not fair.
I am six feet tall.
The soul is so small.
It fits in the palm of my hand.
Shouldn't I pick on someone my own size?
Do I owe the soul an apology?
All right then, I will apologize.
Stupid little soul, I am sorry.
Funny looking little soul, I cannot help myself.
Even now I am laughing at you as you sit in the palm of my hand.
Even as I apologize to you with your silly little hands over your pointy little ears.

EAGLES

A pair of bald eagles
lives on the lake.
I seldom see them.
When I do, it's only one
or the other. But today
I saw both. They soared
in great circles above
me as I walked. They
were high and rising
higher, and their white
heads and white tails
were almost translucent
in the sunlight. They
disappeared in the sun
so that all I saw were
the wings dark in the sky.
Someday I, too, want to
disappear exactly that way.

IN MY DREAM I DID NOT HAVE A NAME

In my dream I did not have a name.
I did not need a name.
I had a face that everyone knew by any other name.
I was *This One.*
I was *That One.*
I was *The Other One.*
I was *You Know Who I Mean.*
I was *Him.*
I was *What's His Name.*
I did not want a name.
I wanted to be known for not having a name.
I wanted to be famous for anonymity.
I wanted to be famous for want of fame.
This was my dream.
This is my dream.

IT IS WARM

It is warm.
It is too warm for February.
The wild cherry tree is next to me.
I reach out to feel its old rough bark.
I feel for the wild cherry tree.
It feels like blossoming.
It feels like booming its white blooms into the world.
I feel it, too.
I feel like blooming my white blooms into the world.
But it is February.
The wild cherry tree will regret it.
I will regret it.
Global warming or no global warming, it is February.
I feel for the wild cherry tree.
We will regret it.

DON'T YOU WANT TO BE READY?

Don't you want to be ready?
Don't you want to be ready for anything?
Don't you want to be ready to leave at a moment's notice?
Don't you want to be ready as ready can be for a novice?
Don't you want to be ready or ready or not?
Don't you want to be steady on your feet?
Don't you want to be steady as they come?
Don't you want to be steady, boys, steady now?
Don't you want to be steady in the face of it?
Don't you want to be steady in the worst place of it?
Don't you want to be a study in steadiness?
Don't you want to be a Hamlet of readiness?
Don't you want to be steady?
Don't you want to be ready?

A TUFTED TITMOUSE

Little lord of the manor,
a tufted titmouse
has the big abandoned
oak tree all to itself.

WAITING IS NOT THE SAME AS WAITING AROUND

Waiting is not the same as waiting around.
The one is living while dying.
The other is dying while living.
But when everything you do
seems like waiting for something else,
then it is time to weigh your time.
It is dying while living, or it is living while dying.
It must be one or the other.
It cannot be both at once.
That is why there is one scale.
That is why there is one weight.
That is why there is one life.
That is why there is one death.

MOE WAS MY FAVORITE STOOGE

Moe was my favorite Stooge.
He was the boss.
He was the brains of the outfit.
He was a more Hitlerish Hitler than Chaplin.
He always had the best looking wife of the three.
Or was that Larry?

THERE WAS ALMOST A WAR

There was almost a war.
That was just one of a thousand.
It came close.
But like the others was averted.
Neither wanted the war.
They all say that.
But both threatened the war.
They all do that.
It was one war, but it seemed like two different wars.
It sounded like two different wars, the way they talked.
But it was one war.
It was one war they both could dare.
It was one war they both could share.
It was one bloody shirt they both could wave.
There was almost a war.
It was averted.
It was close.
It was so close you could smell it.

IF IT WEREN'T FOR IT WAS

If it weren't for it was, I would have gone.
If it weren't for it was, I would have stayed.
If it weren't for it was, I would have spoken.
If it weren't for it was, I would have remained silent.
If it weren't for it was, I would have waved.
If it weren't for it was, I would have gone sooner.
If it weren't for it was, I would have stayed that much longer.
If it weren't for it was, I would have spoken up more truthfully.
If it weren't for it was, I would have remained silent more honestly.
If it weren't for it was, I would have waved less wearily.

A QUESTION

This morning, the flycatchers tied
the sun up in golden knots.

Who will come at dusk
to untie them again?

FROM THE GARDEN

The Black-eyed Susans cry out:
"Look at us!"

While the Shasta daisies,
 just behind,

smile softly and whisper:
"But he will remember us."

THE APPEARANCES

If it appears
you are going
your separate ways,
look again.
You will see
that you are going
the same way
separately.
Look again.
You will see
that you cast
but one shadow.
Look again.
You will see
nothing but
the sun.

IN THE MIDDLE OF THE NIGHT

In the middle of the night,
the train comes, and it comes

with a warning. It says, *Time
passes, or what passes for time,*

*passes. Either way it comes
to the same for both of us.*

*With or without my music.
With or without your words.*

KAFKA'S CANE

No doubt he wanted
it as a complement to his
black suit and bowler hat,
the ones he wore every day,
even in summer. Or maybe
he wanted one because he
recalled that Balzac inscribed
the head of his cane, *I crush
all obstacles*, which he could
now turn on its head into,
All obstacles crush me.
What a comical figure he
must have made walking to
the workmen's compensation
office as, every few steps,
crushed by all obstacles, he
fell to his knees, or on his back,
here he flailed about to right
himself, the cane scribbling
parables in the air.

LAST NIGHT AFTER THE CONCERT

Last night after the concert,
the full moon was so luminous
that had my wife and daughter
not been in the car, I would have
driven home without my headlights.
Instead, I pretended the full moon
was Franz Schubert. Instead, I pretended
my headlights were my useless voice,
joyfully drowned in the light.

THE ONLY SIX-LINE LIMERICK YOU'LL EVER NEED

There once was a turkey named Buck
who fell in love with a duck.
Though he wrote her a sonnet
and bought her a bonnet,
poor Buck with that duck had no luck.
(And I bet you thought I'd say *fuck.*)

FREEDOMLAND

It was in a corner of the Bronx, the hated Yankees borough. It was a theme park built to look like a map of the United States. It closed after a couple of years. I don't know what's there now. I went with my friend Elliot to see Paul Anka. Wait. We hated Paul Anka. We went to check out the girls who went to see Paul Anka. I noticed him standing off to the side of the stage, in the shadows, alone, a big black man with white hair. He was eating a hot dog. I recognized him at once. He was on television a lot in the sixties after he retired because he didn't want to be traded to the Giants. He was active in the civil rights movement. He had family troubles. I don't know why he was there. He must have brought his daughter to see Paul Anka. He did have a daughter. I went up to him while Elliot watched some girls screaming at Paul Anka. I didn't know what to say. I said, *Aren't you Jackie Robinson?* He nodded. He was still eating the hot dog. I put out my hand. He put out his hand. His hand was very large and very callused. My hand disappeared into the fielder's glove of his hand. I didn't know what to say. I said, *How do you like the Dodgers this year? I don't follow baseball anymore*, he said. I didn't know what to say. I said, *Just want to be alone, huh?* He nodded. He threw the napkin in the trash. I didn't know what to say. I said, *Okay.* I walked away. Elliot was standing with some girls without boyfriends. Jackie Robinson was alone again, as he wished to be, in the shadows of a sad, strange place in a corner of the Bronx, the hated Yankees borough, called *Freedomland.* It was torn down soon after. I don't know what's there now.

POEM USING THE RHYMES OF A SONNET BY EDNA ST. VINCENT MILLAY

To a Student Who Asked for My Opinon

Listen, it isn't my intention to offend,
but I have to be honest. (And this implies
that you do too for in the end
that's all there is.) Listen. This enterprise
is not for you. Somewhere along the way you were ill-
advised. Let this horse go – unsaddled, unspurred,
unridden to pasture. Find one of another color. Still,
it's not all bad. Here and there is a word
well chosen. But, of course, there is bound
to be in any poem. This about your girlfriend's knees
is nice. The rest, though, is unformed, unsound,
unsounding unpoetry. So please… Please…
Look. A mercy killing. Turn him on his side,
aim, shoot, and remember why he died.

BLACK-EYED SUSANS

Because the black-eyed Susans
grow where the sun does not go
(because they are blocked by
the maple tree) most of the time,
they make their own sunlight.
They do their best there between
the wrought-iron fence and the maple
tree (they don't quite have the color
right, and each has a mole, dark brown,
at its center). It would be nice if someone
stopped (if only for a moment) to look
at them, but each is intent on getting
straight to the parking lot and then
straight to somewhere else. Nevertheless,
they do their best there, between the maple
tree and the wrought-iron fence.

SOME MYSTERIES ARE DEEPER THAN OTHERS

For Frank Conaway

Forget the rain that morning that closed
off to a drizzle when we got the boat in.
Forget the gray mist and how it rose
from the lake like the ghost of Hamlet's father.
Most of all, forget the great blue heron,
shadow-silent, fishing the opposite shore.
Let's cut to the chase. It was a big one.
That fish was big. That carp was a monster.
I thought the s-o-b was going to pull
us down, floatation cushions, boat and all.
It was big. On eight pound test. Or was it ten?
It was big. No, it was six, and I still
remember how my arm ached for two days after.
Or was it three? It was big. Hell, it was four!

FIELD MOUSE

You would think
he wouldn't stand
a chance, not with
nine cats in the house.
But this one's clever,
or maybe just fast,
both fast and clever
the way he outwitted
and out ran them all,
using their numbers
against them, rounding
the baseboards of
their field, this visitor
in grey, the way
he came back safe
through the hole in
the pantry floor
leaving the home team
standing there, frozen in
position, staring down,
wondering how on
earth they lost.

FEBRUARY

The wild cherry tree
wears the sun
as though it were
its own blossoms,
the branches
practicing for spring.

DO YOU EAT THE SUN FOR BREAKFAST?

Do you eat the sun for breakfast?
The sun is good for breakfast.

Do you eat the clouds for lunch?
The clouds are good for lunch.

Do you eat the moon for dinner?
The moon is bad for dinner.

The moon will give you indigestion.
The moon will give you bad dreams.

SOMEDAY

Someday
the last poet

in the world
will write

the world's
last poem.

This, too,
will be

anonymous.
This, too,

will be in a
dead language.

This, too,
will be

a hymn
to the sun.

ABOUT THE AUTHOR

 J.R. Solonche is the author of nineteen books of poetry and coauthor of another. He lives in the Hudson Valley.

CPSIA information can be obtained
at www.ICGtesting.com
Printed in the USA
BVHW032150141020
591097BV00001B/90

9 781947 175358